AUG 1 3 2020

CURIOUS

Questions and answers about...

Animals

Words by Camilla de la Bédoyère

Illustrations by Pauline Reeves

WINDMILL BOOKS ™

You're a curious animal, too, so we want to find out about YOU!

What's your NAME?

How OLD are you?

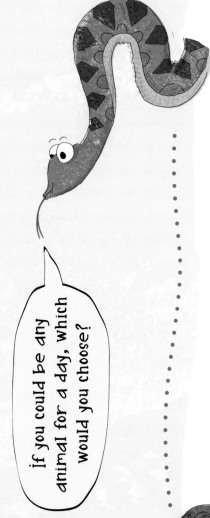

If you could be any animal for a day, which would you choose?

Published in 2020 by Windmill Books,
an Imprint of Rosen Publishing
29 East 21st Street, New York, NY 10010

Copyright © 2020 Miles Kelly Publishing

Cataloging-in-Publication Data

Names: De la Bédoyère, Camilla. | Reeves, Pauline.
Title: Animals / Camilla de la Bédoyère, illustrated by Pauline Reeves.
Description: New York : Windmill Books, 2020. | Series: Curious questions and answers about...
Identifiers: ISBN 9781725394919 (pbk.) | ISBN 9781725394933 (library bound) | ISBN 9781725394926 (6 pack) | ISBN 9781725394940 (ebook)
Subjects: LCSH: Animals--Encyclopedias--Juvenile literature. | Children's questions and answers--Juvenile literature.
Classification: LCC QL49.D3738 2020 | DDC 590.3--dc23

Manufactured in the United States of America

CPSIA Compliance Information: Batch BW20WM: For Further Information contact Rosen Publishing, New York, New York at 1-800-237-9932

Are you an early bird or a night owl?

CURIOUS
questions and answers about...
Animals

What's your favorite color?

Words by Camilla de la Bédoyère

Illustrations by Pauline Reeves

Do you like warm weather better, or snow?

If you could eat one food every day, what would it be?

If you could have any animal for a pet, which would you choose?

What's your FAVORITE animal?

WINDMILL BOOKS ™

What Is an Animal?

Animals are living things that do all of these things...

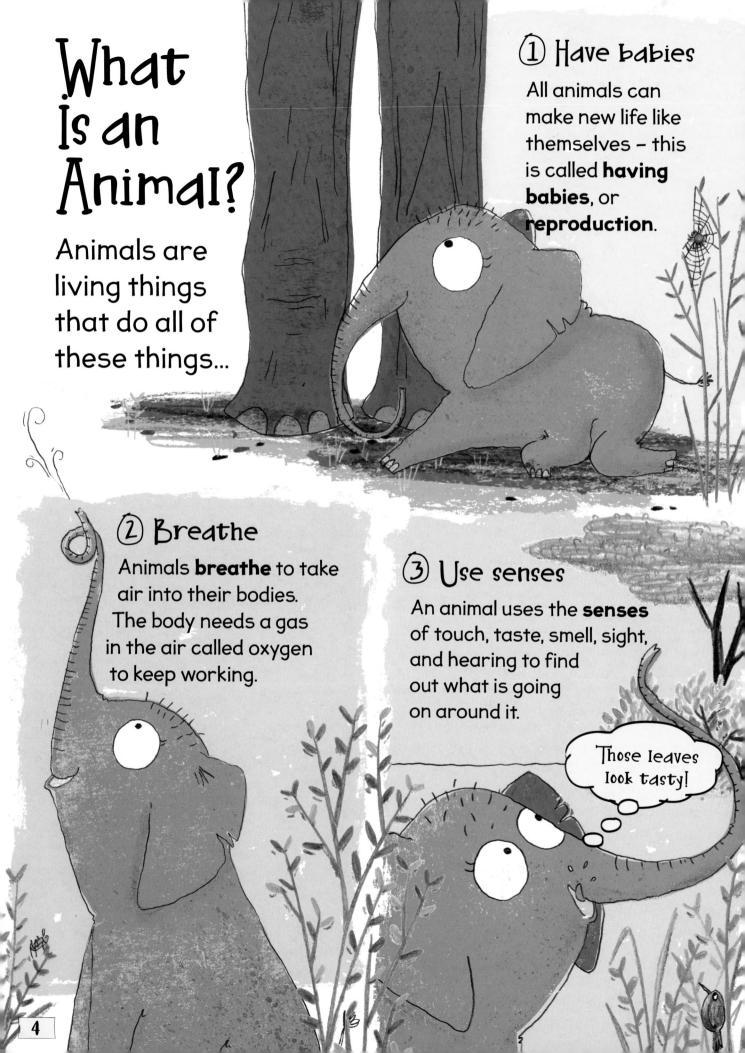

① Have babies

All animals can make new life like themselves – this is called **having babies**, or **reproduction**.

② Breathe

Animals **breathe** to take air into their bodies. The body needs a gas in the air called oxygen to keep working.

③ Use senses

An animal uses the **senses** of touch, taste, smell, sight, and hearing to find out what is going on around it.

Those leaves look tasty!

④ Move

Most animals **move** to get to food and water, to find safe places, and to escape from danger.

I learned to stand up 30 minutes after I was born. How old were you when you learned to stand?

⑤ Eat

Animals must **eat** food to stay alive. Food gives them energy so they can **move** and **grow**.

Munch!

⑥ Get rid of waste

Waste is leftover food that an animal's body doesn't need.

Waste not, want not! Dung beetles like me use elephant poop for lots of things!

⑦ Grow

All animals start small and **grow** bigger until they are old enough to **have babies** of their own.

Why Do Crocodiles Eat Stones?

Because they swallow their meaty meals whole, and the stones help to grind up the food in their tummies!

Crocs are one of the world's biggest carnivores, or meat eaters. We eat fish, birds, rats, snakes, lizards, and even deer and pigs.

What makes flamingos pink?

Flamingos are pink because they eat pink shrimp that live in VERY salty lakes! They feed with their heads upside down.

Can you see any other upside-down eaters around here?

Who likes eating greens?

Leaves and other greens taste great to herbivores (plant eaters) like sloths. Some greens are tough to eat, so they spend lots of time chewing.

Anteaters like me eat ants and termites – thousands of them every day! We lick them up with our long, sticky tongues.

Are animals picky eaters?

They can be! Some only eat one special food. Others, like tiger sharks and brown bears, will eat almost anything they can find!

What Are Senses?

Senses are the body's way of finding out about the world. Animals use senses to locate food, find their way around, avoid danger, and make friends. The five main senses are **hearing**, **sight**, **smell**, **taste**, and **touch**.

HEARING

Ear

Do bugs have ears?

Yes — lots of bugs can hear better than humans, but our ears can be in strange places! I'm a bush cricket, and my ears are on my legs.

What are whiskers for?

TOUCH

A cat's whiskers are very sensitive. I use them to feel things — they can tell me if a space I want to crawl into is too small for my body.

How do snakes smell?

Snakes can smell with their tongues. They flick them in the air to detect any appealing odors!

SMELL

TASTE

Why is it a bad idea to lick a frog?

i make a foul-tasting slime in my skin. it stops animals from eating me.

SIGHT

Do all animals have two eyes?

Some animals have more than two! Most spiders have eight eyes, but cave spiders have none. They live in caves where it's always dark.

Did You Know?

A **fulmar** is a foul seabird. It spits a stinky oil at anyone who gets too close.

The **giraffe** is the tallest animal that lives on land.

Lobsters have blue blood and some dogs have blue tongues.

When a **sand tiger shark** wants to sink to the seabed, it has to burp first!

A spiny **sea urchin** is covered in tiny feet. Its mouth is on its bottom!

Mimic octopuses can change shape and color. They can pretend to be fish or sea snakes.

Sweat bees like the smell and taste of human sweat!

If a **sponge** is broken into bits, this strange sea creature is able to put itself back together again!

The **dung beetle** is the strongest animal on Earth. If it were the size of a human, it could pull six buses full of people!

A **spider** eats about 2,000 bugs a year.

Australian **burrowing frogs** cover themselves in slime, so when flies land on them they get stuck – and the frogs can gobble them up.

Bees wag their bottoms in a crazy dance to tell each other where to find the best flowers.

Hippos don't just yawn when they are tired – they also yawn when they are angry or scared.

A **blue whale** eats millions of pink shrimp, so its poop is pink, too. Each poop can be bigger than you!

A **catfish** can use its whole body to taste. Its skin is covered with taste buds.

What's Inside an Animal?

If you had to build an animal from scratch, here's what you would need...

Spine

① Framework

Most big animals have a **skeleton**, a framework of bones beneath their skin. Smaller animals have a tough outside – like a shell or strong skin – called an **exoskeleton**.

Ribs

③ Inner workings

Soft, squishy body parts called organs do useful jobs such as thinking, breathing, and turning food into energy.

Brain

Tail

Lung

Liver

Heart

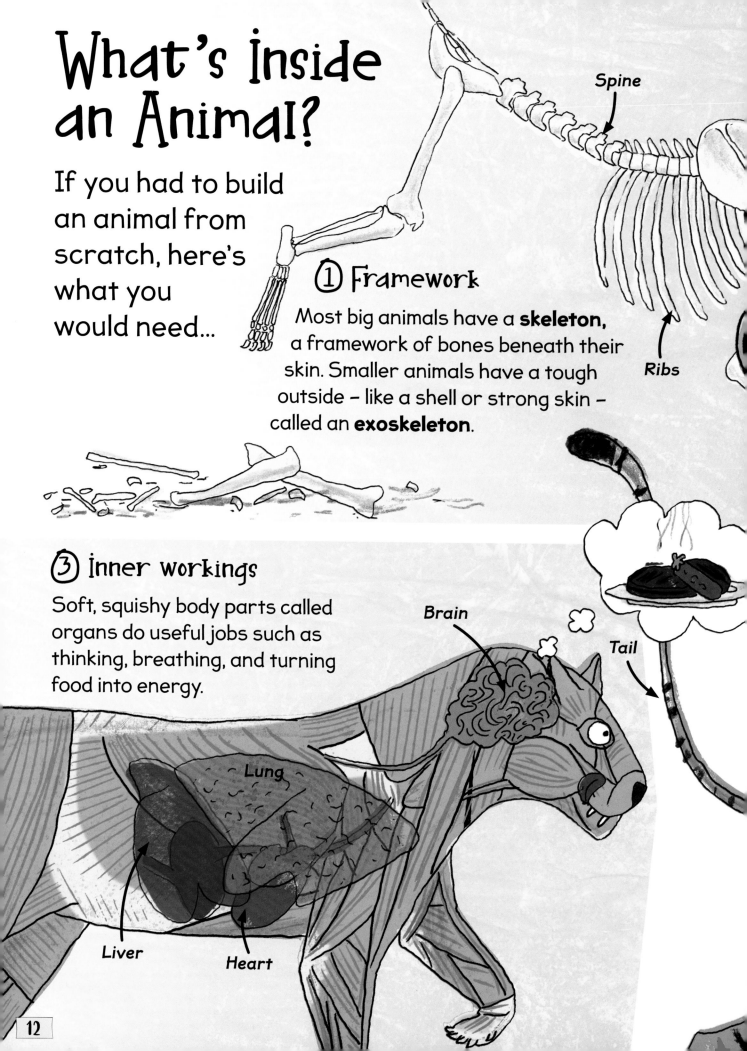

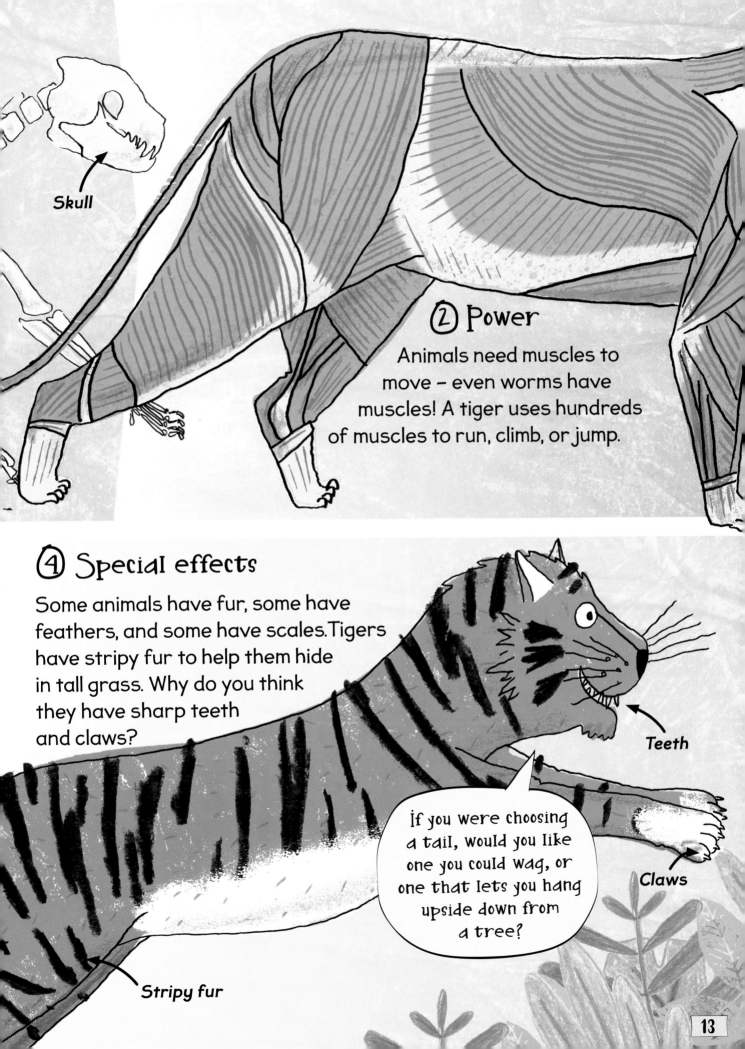

Skull

② Power

Animals need muscles to move – even worms have muscles! A tiger uses hundreds of muscles to run, climb, or jump.

④ Special effects

Some animals have fur, some have feathers, and some have scales. Tigers have stripy fur to help them hide in tall grass. Why do you think they have sharp teeth and claws?

Teeth

If you were choosing a tail, would you like one you could wag, or one that lets you hang upside down from a tree?

Claws

Stripy fur

Why Are You Blue?

Colors and patterns make an animal beautiful! They can also make an animal look scary, or help it to hide.

Blue-ringed octopus

My color is a sign of danger. When I'm scared, blue circles appear on my skin. They are a warning that i can kill any attackers with venom.

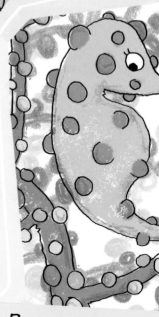

Blue morpho butterfly

Danger or disguise?

Some animals blend into the background. This is called camoflage. Others have colors and patterns that warn enemies to stay away. Which of these creatures are using camouflage, and which are using warning colors?

Strawberry poison dart frog

Pygmy seahorse

My colors help me hide. A blue or dark gray shark can prowl through the sea, unseen by the fish it is looking for.

Blue shark

Would you rather have blue feet, like me, or a blue bottom, like a baboon?

Southern crowned-pigeon

Blue-footed booby

My beautiful blue feathers make me look healthy and fit to attract a mate.

Leaf insect

Banded sea krait

Lion

Would You Rather?

Winter is coming! Would you prefer to travel to somewhere warm, like a **sand martin**, or curl up and sleep through it, like a **dormouse**?

Would you rather be spotted like a **leopard**, or striped like a **tiger**?

ZZzzz...

Is it better to have a long neck, like a **giraffe**...

...or lots of arms, like an **octopus**?

You look soooo cute!

A giraffe uses its long neck to reach leaves in tall trees. An octopus uses its arms to move, touch, taste, and gather food.

If you were an animal baby, would you prefer to sit in dad's pouch, like a **seahorse**, or in mom's, like a **kangaroo**?

It's picnic time! Would you prefer to dig into a rotting dead animal, like a **vulture**, or suck down some animal poop, like a **sea cucumber**?

Erm... yummy?

Would you rather have armor, like a **pangolin**, or spikes, like a **pufferfish**?

WHOOSH!

Would you rather be able to dive through the air at 125 miles (200 km) per hour, like a **peregrine falcon**, or fly 9,320 miles (15,000 km) in a single journey, like an **albatross**?

Is it better to be best friends with a **shark** or a **crocodile**?

Sharks and crocodiles are both big carnivores. That means they eat other animals, so it's probably not a good idea to try to make friends with either!

Will you play with me?

Why Do Spiders Do Cartwheels?

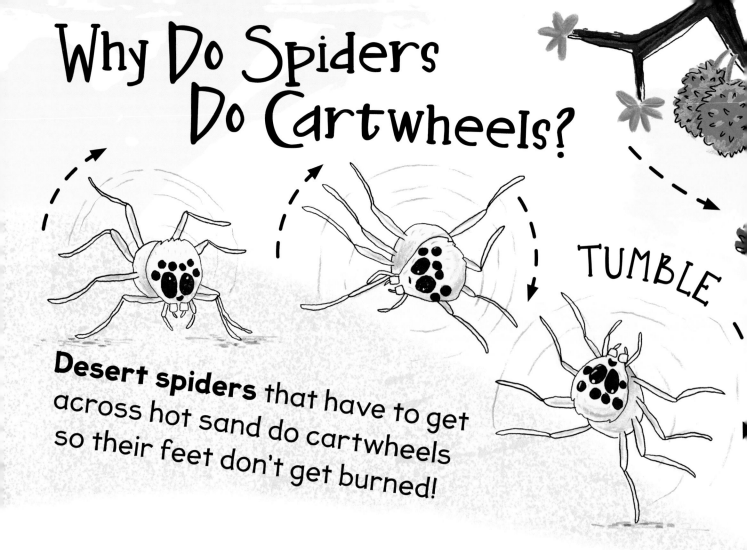

TUMBLE

Desert spiders that have to get across hot sand do cartwheels so their feet don't get burned!

How high can you jump?

BOUNCE

LEAP

Kangaroos can jump up to 10 feet (3 m) into the air, but we can't walk or move backwards.

Why do orangutans have long arms?

Long arms are great for swinging through trees. We also have hands for gripping branches and grabbing fruit.

SWING

Antelopes leap several yards at a time, springing up in the air to escape from danger.

Which bird flies, but goes nowhere?

HOVER

A hummingbird does. It flaps and twists its wings so that it can hover in front of a flower, where it drinks the sweet nectar.

I can leap more than 100 times my own height.

SPRING

Fleas jump so they can leap from animal to animal, where they suck blood!

19

How fast do cheetahs sprint?

A cheetah is the fastest running animal on the planet. It can reach top speeds of over 60 miles (100 km) an hour.

① Built for speed

A cheetah's body is packed with small but powerful muscles.

Why Do Cheetahs Run Fast?

Like many hunters, cheetahs turn on the speed when they want to catch their lunch! The antelope they chase need to be fast, too, if they hope to escape.

Why are tortoises so slow?

Tortoises plod along slowly because they don't need speed to catch their lunch – they eat grass! They don't need to be fast to escape from danger, either, because their tough shells protect them like a suit of armor.

② Big strides

It has a very bendy spine and long, slim legs.

③ Long leap

All four of a cheetah's feet leave the ground as it runs.

Why do crabs run sideways?

Because the way their legs bend means they can't run forward!

Is that a statue?

During the day, a potoo bird doesn't move at all! It pretends to be a branch. At night, it flies around, hunting bugs to eat.

How Many?

An octopus has **3** hearts but an earthworm has **5**.

A squid has **2** tentacles...

... and it has **8** arms.

Sea otters have **800 million** hairs on their bodies.

Tree kangaroos can jump **100** feet (30 m) from a tree to the ground below.

A snow leopard can leap more than **33** feet (10 m) in a single bound.

A snake can live for up to **6** months without eating.

A giraffe's tongue is **18** inches (45 cm) long.

20 The number of hours three-toed sloths, koalas, and lions might sleep in one day.

310,700

The number of miles a sooty tern can fly without stopping for a rest.

Monarch butterflies can go on incredible journeys – one butterfly flew more than **2,500** miles (4,025 km) to lay its eggs!

4

The number of wings a bee has.

1

The number of hours it takes a snail to slime its way along just **3** feet of ground.

The largest number of legs ever counted on a millipede.

750

A mother cane toad can lay **35,000** eggs at a time.

14

The length, in inches, of the longest insect – a type of stick insect called Chan's megastick.

Is Anyone at Home?

Yes! An animal's home is a safe place where it can look after its babies. Animal homes are called habitats. They can be as big as an ocean or as small as a single leaf.

Froghopper nest

Who lives in a home made of spit?

Young froghopper insects build a home of froth around themselves! This "spit" keeps them safe while they grow.

Why do frogs like water?

Because they need to lay their eggs in it. They are amphibians, which means they can live in water or on land.

Some animals that live in or near water have to come up to the surface to breathe air.

Others have gills and breathe underwater.

Frogs like to live in wet places

Birds nest in tree branches

Owls and their chicks live in tree holes

Why do owls hoot?

They hoot to tell other owls to stay away from their tree. Some animals don't like neighbors!

This fox den is under the tree's roots

Ladybugs also lay their eggs on leaves

Would you rather live in a treetop nest with chicks, or in an underground sett with badger cubs?

Can Animals Make Things?

Yes, some animals are expert builders and can make super structures.

① *A hoop of grass...*

② *...turns into a ball...*

③ *...and then a home.*

Which bird builds the best nest?

A dad weaver bird makes his nest by stitching blades of grass together, then stuffing feathers inside to make a soft bed. He sings to tell mom she can lay her eggs there.

① *Strong silk makes the frame*

② *Sticky silk is used in the spiral*

Why do spiders build webs?

So they can trap flies. A spider makes the silk in its body and then spins it into a web.

Who loves mud?

Millions of termites do! They build their huge, towering homes from mud. A group of termites that live together is called a colony, and their home can last for years.

There are passages, tunnels, and places to store food inside

HOME SWEET HOME

A termite mound can be more than 7 feet (2 m) high!

A single queen lays all the eggs

What's the Point of Moms and Dads?

Some animal babies look after themselves, but many need moms and dads to give them food and keep them safe.

Where do penguins keep their eggs?

Emperor penguins like us keep our eggs off the ice by holding them on our feet. The skin on our tummies is covered with fluffy feathers to keep our chicks warm.

How does a baby orca sleep?

Baby orcas can swim as soon as they are born, and they sleep while they are swimming! Orcas can rest one half of their brain at a time. The other half stays wide awake.

A baby orca is called a calf

Do baby animals drink milk?

Yes, furry animals are called mammals and they feed their babies with milk. A polar bear mom looks after her cubs in a snowy den during the long, cold winter.

ZZZZZZ

Would you rather have an orca, a penguin, or a polar bear for a parent?

A Compendium of Questions

Are sharks the most dangerous animals?

Sharks don't usually attack people. Snakes, donkeys, and dogs hurt people more often than sharks!

Can a lizard run across water?

A basilisk lizard can. It runs really fast and uses its big feet and tail to help it balance on top of the water.

How does a squid escape from a hungry shark?

A squid squirts jets of water, and zooms off! The jets of water push the squid forward. This is called jet propulsion.

Why do jellyfish wobble?

Jellyfish don't have any bones and their bodies are full of water!

Do all animals have bones?

Mammals, birds, reptiles, amphibians, and fish have bones. All other animals – including bugs, crabs, and octopuses – don't.

What is venom?

Venom is a poison. Venomous animals can inject it using their fangs, claws, spines, or stingers. They use it to defend themselves, or to kill animals for food.

Is a bat a bird?

No, it's a flying mammal. Bats are the only mammals that fly.

How do animals glide?

Gliding lizards, frogs, and squirrels have large flaps of skin that they stretch out before they leap from a tree. The skin works like a parachute to help them glide and land softly.

Do camels keep water in their humps?

No – a camel's hump is full of fat, not water.

Do lions purr?

Big cats roar but can't purr, and small cats purr but can't roar. Big cats sometimes make a noise like a growly purr!

What's the smallest bird?

A bee hummingbird. It's smaller than your thumb. An ostrich is the biggest bird.

How many animals are in the world?

No one knows, but there are billions of ants, so it must be lots!

Glossary

compendium: a collection of things gathered together and presented as a group

disguise: the state of having a false appearance

dormouse: an animal, found in Europe, Asia, and Africa, that looks like a small squirrel

oxygen: a colorless, odorless gas that animals, including people, need to breathe

passage: a narrow space things or animals can move through

Index